Fun Colorful
Quilts

MW00594256

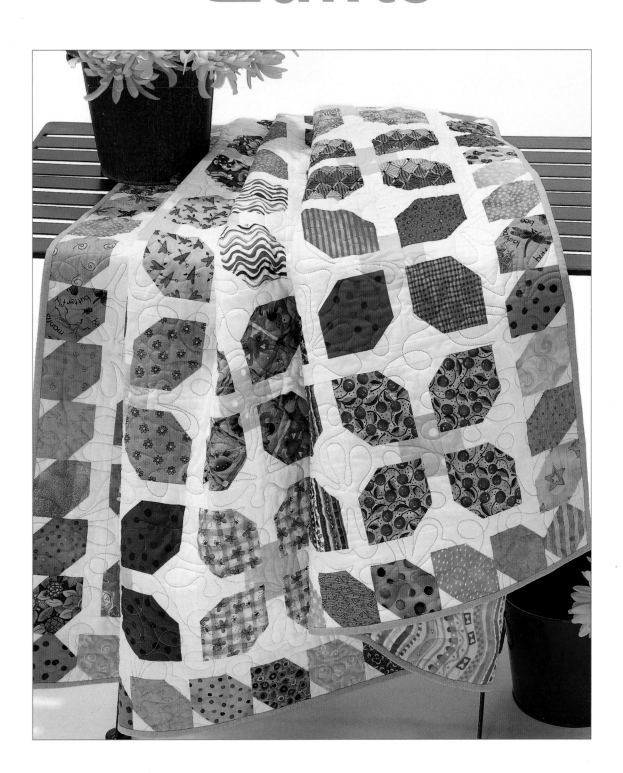

LEISURE ARTS, INC. • Maumelle, Arkansas

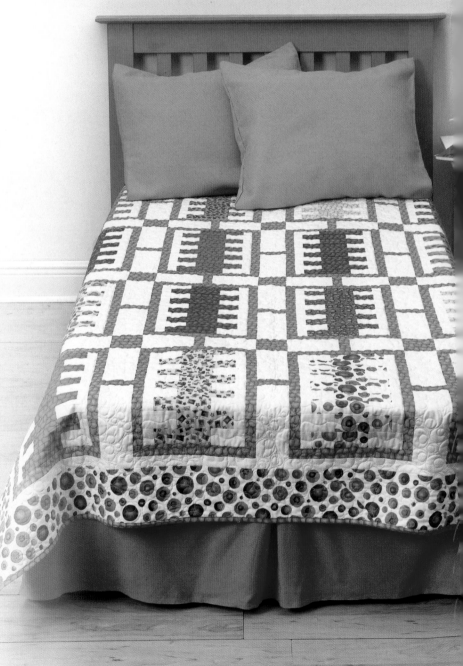

EDITORIAL STAFF

Senior Product Director: Pam Stebbins

Creative Art Director: Katherine Laughlin

Publications Director: Leah Lampirez

Technical Editors: Lisa Lancaster and Jean Lewis

Editorial Writer: Susan Frantz Wiles

Art Category Manager: Lora Puls

Graphic Artist: Jessica Bramlett

Prepress Technician: Stephanie Johnson

BUSINESS STAFF

President and Chief Executive Officer: Fred F. Pruss

Senior Vice President of Operations: Jim Dittrich

Vice President of Retail Sales: Martha Adams

Chief Financial Officer: Tiffany P. Childers

Controller: Teresa Eby

Information Technology Director: Brian Roden

Director of E-Commerce: Mark Hawkins

Manager of E-Commerce: Robert Young

Vibrant fabrics in a medley of popular shapes, from circles and stars to squares and triangles, make these quilts fun and colorful.

ISBN-13/EAN: 978-1-4647-3532-5
UPC: 0-28906-06481-0

CONTENTS

PETAL PUSHERS

Finished Quilt Size: 73" x 73" (185 cm x 185 cm)
Finished Block Size: 8¹/₈" x 8¹/₈" (21 cm x 21 cm)

SHOPPING LIST

Yardage is based on 43"/44" (109 cm/112 cm) wide fabric with a usable width of 40" (102 cm) after trimming selvages and shrinkage.

- ☐ 2¹/₂ yds (2.3 m) **total** of assorted print fabrics
- ☐ ⁵/₈ yd (57 cm) of yellow print fabric
- ☐ 3⁷/₈ yds (3.5 m) of white solid fabric
- ☐ 1 yd (91 cm) **total** of assorted green print fabrics
- ☐ 4¹/₂ yds (4.1 m) of fabric for backing
- ☐ ⁵/₈ yd (57 cm) of fabric for binding

You will also need:

- ☐ 81" x 81" (206 cm x 206 cm) square of batting

Design by Me & My Sister Designs
Barbara Groves and Mary Jacobson

CUTTING THE PIECES

*Follow **Rotary Cutting**, page 37, to cut fabric. All measurements include ¹/₄" seam allowances.*

From assorted print fabrics:
- • Cut 49 sets of 4 matching **squares** 4" x 4" (**A**).

From yellow print fabric:
- • Cut 5 **strips** 1⁵/₈" wide (**B**).
- • Cut 3 **strips** 3⁷/₈" wide (**C**).

From white solid fabric:
- • Cut 11 **strips** 2⁷/₈" wide (**D**).
- • Cut 27 strips 1³/₄" wide. From these strips, cut 584 **squares** 1³/₄" x 1³/₄" (**E**).
- • Cut 29 strips 1⁵/₈" wide. From 11 of these strips, cut 42 **short sashings** 1⁵/₈" x 8⁵/₈" (**F**). Leave 18 strips (**G**) uncut.

From assorted green print fabrics:
- • Cut 92 **squares** 3¹/₂" x 3¹/₂" (**H**).

From fabric for binding:
- • Cut 8 **binding strips** 2¹/₄" wide (**I**).

ASSEMBLING THE BLOCKS

*Follow **Piecing**, page 38, and **Pressing**, page 39. Measurements given throughout assembly include outer seam allowances. Use a 1/4" seam allowance throughout.*

1. Draw a diagonal line (corner to corner) on wrong side of each **square (E)**. With right sides together, place a **square (E)** on opposite corners of a **square (A)**. Stitch seam on marked line. Set aside remaining **squares (E)**.

2. Trim seam allowance to 1/4" **(Fig. 1)** and press open to make **Unit 1**. Unit 1 should measure 4" x 4". Make 49 sets of 4 matching **Unit 1's**.

Fig. 1

Unit 1 (make 49 sets of 4 matching)

3. Sew 1 **strip (B)** and 1 **strip (D)** together to make **Strip Set A**. Make 5 Strip Set A's. Cut across Strip Set A's at 1⁵/₈" intervals to make **Unit 2**. Unit 2 should measure 1⁵/₈" x 4". Make 98 Unit 2's.

Strip Set A (make 5)   Unit 2 (make 98)

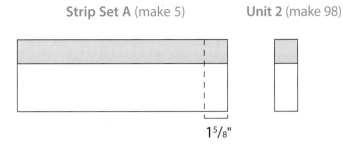

1⁵/₈"

4. Sew 1 **strip (D)** to each side of 1 **strip (C)** to make **Strip Set B**. Make 3 Strip Set B's. Cut across Strip Set B's at 1⁵/₈" intervals to make **Unit 3**. Unit 3 should measure 1⁵/₈" x 8⁵/₈". Make 49 Unit 3's.

Strip Set B (make 3)   Unit 3 (make 49)

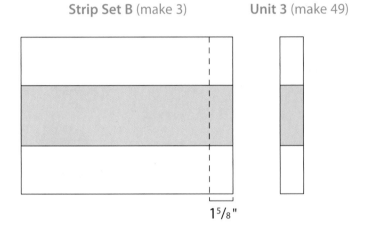

1⁵/₈"

5. Sew 2 matching **Unit 1's** and 1 **Unit 2** together to make **Unit 4**. Unit 4 should measure 8⁵/₈" x 4". Make 98 Unit 4's.

Unit 4 (make 98)

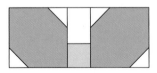

6. Sew 1 **Unit 3** and 2 matching **Unit 4's** together to make **Flower Block**. Flower Block should measure 8⅝" x 8⅝". Make 49 Flower Blocks.

Flower Block (make 49)

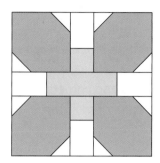

ASSEMBLING THE QUILT TOP CENTER

*Refer to **Quilt Top Diagram**, page 9, for placement.*

1. Sew 7 **Flower Blocks** and 6 **short sashings (F)** together to make a **Row**. A Row should measure 64⅛" x 8⅝". Make 7 Rows.

Row (make 7)

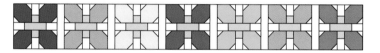

2. Using diagonal seams (**Fig. 2**), sew 11 **strips (G)** together end to end to make 1 continuous length. From this length, cut 6 **long sashings** 1⅝" x 64⅛".

Fig. 2

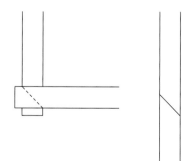

3. Sew 7 **Rows** and 6 **long sashings** together to make **Quilt Top Center**. The Quilt Top Center should measure 64⅛" x 64⅛".

ADDING THE BORDERS

Inner Borders

1. Using diagonal seams (**Fig. 2**), sew 7 **strips (G)** together end to end to make 1 continuous inner border strip.
2. To determine length of **inner side borders**, measure length across center of quilt top center. From continuous inner border strip, cut 2 **inner side borders** the determined length. Matching centers and corners, sew **inner side borders** to quilt top center.
3. To determine length of **inner top/bottom borders**, measure width across center of quilt top center (including added borders). From continuous inner border strip, cut 2 **inner top/bottom borders** the determined length. Matching centers and corners, sew **inner top/bottom borders** to quilt top center.

Outer Borders

1. With right sides together, place a white **square (E)** on opposite corners of a **square (H)**. Stitch seam on marked line.
2. Trim seam allowance to ¼" (**Fig. 3**) and press open to make **Leaf Block**. Leaf Block should measure 3½" x 3½". Make 92 Leaf Blocks.

Fig. 3

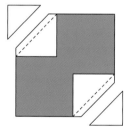

Leaf Block (make 92)

3. With right sides together, place a white **square** (E) on each remaining corner of 4 **Leaf Blocks**. Stitch seam on marked line.

4. Trim seam allowance to $^1/4$" **(Fig. 4)** and press open to make **Cornerstone Block**. Cornerstone Block should measure $3^1/2$" x $3^1/2$". Make 4 **Cornerstone Blocks**.

5. Sew 22 **Leaf Blocks** together to make **Outer Border**. Adjust Outer Border length to measure $66^3/8$" long by taking smaller or larger seam allowances as needed. Make 4 Outer Borders.

6. Matching centers and corners, sew 1 **Outer Border** to each side of quilt top.

7. Sew a **Cornerstone Block** to each end of remaining **Outer Borders**.

8. Matching centers and corners, sew 1 **Outer Border** to top and bottom of quilt top.

Fig. 4

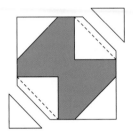

Cornerstone Block (make 4)

COMPLETING THE QUILT

1. Follow **Quilting**, page 41, to mark, layer, and quilt as desired. Our quilt is machine quilted with meandering loops and free-motion dragonflies.
2. Refer to **Making a Hanging Sleeve**, page 45, to make and attach a hanging sleeve, if desired.
3. Follow **Binding**, page 45, to bind quilt using **binding strips (I)**.

Quilt Top Diagram

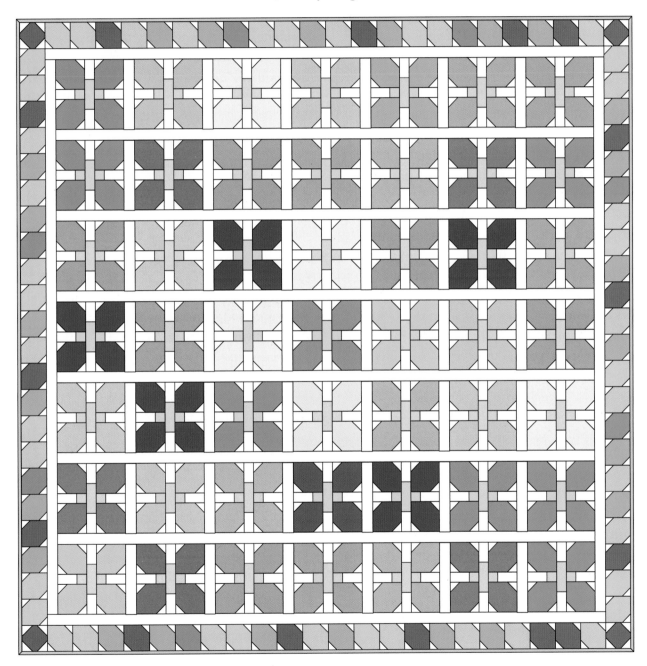

ON A ROLL

Finished Quilt Size: 73" x 87" (185 cm x 221 cm)

SHOPPING LIST

Yardage is based on 43"/44" (109 cm/112 cm) wide fabric with a usable width of 40" (102 cm) after trimming selvages and shrinkage.

- ☐ 3$1/2$ yds (3.2 m) of white print
- ☐ 1$3/4$ yds (1.6 m) of navy print (includes binding)
- ☐ $5/8$ yd (57 cm) of medium green print (Green Print 1)
- ☐ $1/2$ yd (46 cm) of dark green print (Green Print 2)
- ☐ $3/8$ yd (34 cm) *each* of 2 additional green prints (Green Prints 3 and 4)
- ☐ $1/2$ yd (46 cm) of dark orange print (Orange Print 1)
- ☐ $3/8$ yd (34 cm) *each* of 3 additional orange prints (Orange Prints 2, 3, and 4)
- ☐ $1/2$ yd (46 cm) of dark red print (Red Print 1)
- ☐ $3/8$ yd (34 cm) *each* of 3 additional red prints (Red Prints 2, 3, and 4)
- ☐ 1$1/8$ yds (1 m) of dark yellow print (Yellow Print 1)
- ☐ $3/8$ yd (34 cm) *each* of 3 additional yellow prints (Yellow Prints 2, 3, and 4)
- ☐ 6$3/4$ yds (6.2 m) of fabric for backing

You will also need:
- ☐ Template plastic
- ☐ Fine-point permanent marker
- ☐ Fabric marking pencil
- ☐ 2$1/2$ yds (2.3 m) of paper-backed fusible web
- ☐ Stabilizer
- ☐ 81" x 95" (206 cm x 241 cm) rectangle of batting

Design by Tammy Tadd
Quilt made by Velda Grubbs
Machine quilting by Sherry Massey of The Quilter's Loft

CUTTING THE PIECES

*Follow **Rotary Cutting**, page 37, to cut fabric. Follow **Template Cutting**, page 38, to cut template pieces, pages 17 and 19. All measurements include $1/4$" seam allowances. Cut lengths for borders 1, 2, 4, and 5 are exact. You may wish to allow an extra 2" in length for "insurance" and then trim the borders to fit when you add them to the quilt top center.*

White Print
- Cut 1 **rectangle** 33" x 47".
- Cut 6 strips 7$1/2$" wide. Sew these strips together end to end, and then cut 4 **strips** 7$1/2$" x 50$1/2$".
- Cut 8 **strips** 2$1/2$" wide.

Navy Print
- Cut 5 strips 2$1/2$" wide. Sew these strips together end to end, and then cut the following strips:
  - 2 **strips** 2$1/2$" x 46$1/2$".
  - 2 **strips** 2$1/2$" x 36$1/2$".
- Cut 8 **strips** 2$1/2$" wide.
- Cut 1 strip 4$1/2$" wide. From this strip, cut:
  - 4 **squares** 4$1/2$" x 4$1/2$".
  - 4 **squares** 2$1/2$" x 2$1/2$".
- Cut 9 **binding strips** 2" wide.

Green Print 1
- Cut 7 strips 1$1/2$" wide. Sew these strips together end to end and then cut the following strips:
  - 2 **strips** 1$1/2$" x 72$1/2$".
  - 2 **strips** 1$1/2$" x 60$1/2$".
- Cut 2 strips 4$1/2$" wide. From these strips, cut the following pieces:
  - 6 **template A's**.
  - 9 **rectangles** 2$1/2$" x 4$1/2$".

Green Print 2

- Cut 2 strips 4^1/$_2$" wide. From these strips, cut the following pieces:
    - 6 **template A's**.
    - 9 **rectangles** 2^1/$_2$" x 4^1/$_2$".
- Cut 1 **strip** 6^1/$_2$" wide. Later, you will cut template pieces for fusible appliqué from this strip.

Green Prints 3 and 4

- From each fabric, cut 2 strips 4^1/$_2$" wide. From these strips, cut the following pieces:
    - 6 **template A's**.
    - 9 **rectangles** 2^1/$_2$" x 4^1/$_2$".

Orange Print 1

- Cut 2 strips 4^1/$_2$" wide. From these strips, cut the following pieces:
    - 6 **template A's**.
    - 9 **rectangles** 2^1/$_2$" x 4^1/$_2$".
- Cut 1 **strip** 6^1/$_2$" wide. Later, you will cut template pieces for fusible appliqué from this strip.

Orange Prints 2, 3, and 4

- From each fabric, cut 2 strips 4^1/$_2$" wide. From these strips, cut the following pieces:
    - 6 **template A's**.
    - 8 **rectangles** 2^1/$_2$" x 4^1/$_2$".

Red Print 1

- Cut 2 strips 4^1/$_2$" wide. From these strips, cut the following pieces:
    - 6 **template A's**.
    - 10 **rectangles** 2^1/$_2$" x 4^1/$_2$".
- Cut 1 strip 6^1/$_2$" wide. From this strip, cut 4 **squares** 4^1/$_2$" x 4^1/$_2$". Later, you will cut template pieces for fusible appliqué from the remaining portion of this strip.

Red Prints 2, 3, and 4

- From each fabric, cut 2 strips 4^1/$_2$" wide. From these strips, cut the following pieces:
    - 6 **template A's**.
    - 9 **rectangles** 2^1/$_2$" x 4^1/$_2$".

Yellow Print 1

- Cut 2 strips 4^1/$_2$" wide. From these strips, cut the following pieces:
    - 4 **template A's**.
    - 9 **rectangles** 2^1/$_2$" x 4^1/$_2$".
- Cut 1 **strip** 6^1/$_2$" wide. Later, you will cut template pieces for fusible appliqué from this strip.
- Cut 7 strips 2^1/$_2$" wide. Piece these strips together end to end and then cut the following strips:
    - 2 **strips** 2^1/$_2$" x 74^1/$_2$".
    - 2 **strips** 2^1/$_2$" x 60^1/$_2$".

Yellow Prints 2, 3, and 4

- From each fabric, cut 2 strips 4^1/$_2$" wide. From these strips, cut the following pieces:
    - 4 **template A's**.
    - 9 **rectangles** 2^1/$_2$" x 4^1/$_2$".

ASSEMBLING THE QUILT TOP CENTER

*Use ^{1}/$_4$" seam allowances throughout for piecing the candy circles. Follow **Piecing**, page 38, and **Pressing**, page 39, to make the quilt top.*

Make the Candy Circles

You'll need the following candy circles for the quilt top center:

- 2 green candy circles.
- 2 orange candy circles.
- 2 red candy circles.
- 1 yellow candy circle.

1. Select 2 **template A's** from each of the 4 prints of 1 color (for example, 2 each of the 4 green prints).
2. Matching right sides, sew 2 template A's together (use different prints) along one straight edge to make Unit 1. Make 4 Unit 1's.

Unit 1 (make 4)

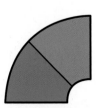

Prepare Templates B, C, and D for Fusible Appliqué

1. Place paper-backed fusible web, paper side up, over template B. Trace template B twice onto the paper side of the web.
2. Follow the manufacturer's instructions to fuse the traced template B to the wrong side of a 6½" wide green print 2 **strip**.
3. Use scissors to cut out template B along the traced lines. Remove the paper backing.
4. Repeat Steps 1-3 to prepare the following additional templates for fusible appliqué.

Fabric	Template
green print 2	1 template C 1 template D
orange print 1	2 template B 1 template C 1 template D
red print 1	2 template B 1 template C 1 template D
yellow print 1	1 template B 1 template C 1 template D

3. Sew Unit 1's together until you have a complete circle (**Fig. 1**). Press seam allowances in one direction.

Fig. 1

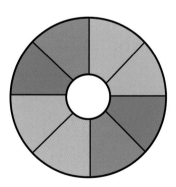

4. Repeat Steps 1-3 to make the 6 remaining candy circles for the quilt top center.

Appliqué the Candy Circles to the Quilt Top Center

*Follow **Satin Stitch Appliqué**, page 40, to appliqué the circles to the quilt center.*

1. Referring to the **Quilt Top Center** diagram for placement, pin the 7 candy circles in place on the 33" x 47" white print **rectangle**. *(Note: After appliquéing, the rectangle will be trimmed. Be sure your appliqués are inside a 32" x 46" area.)* Satin Stitch appliqué the outer edge of each candy circle to the rectangle.

2. Referring to the **Quilt Top Center** diagram for placement, position 1 B in place over a candy circle in the corresponding color (for example, a green B over a green candy circle). Follow the manufacturer's instructions to fuse B in place. Repeat for the remaining candy circles.

3. Satin Stitch appliqué the inner and outer edges of each fused B to the candy circles.

Quilt Top Center

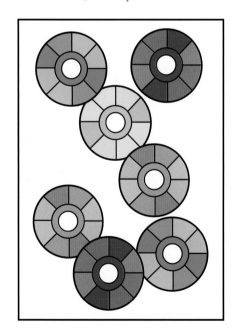

ASSEMBLING THE QUILT BORDERS

Your quilt has 6 borders:
- Navy print inner border (border 1)
- White print border with appliqués (border 2)
- Checkerboard border with corner blocks (border 3)
- Green print border (border 4)
- Yellow print border with corner blocks (border 5)
- Pieced outer border with corner blocks (border 6)

Assemble Border 1

1. Trim the quilt top center to $32^{1}/_{2}$" x $46^{1}/_{2}$".
2. Sew the $2^{1}/_{2}$" x $46^{1}/_{2}$" navy print **border strips** to the long sides of the quilt top center.
3. Sew the $2^{1}/_{2}$" x $36^{1}/_{2}$" navy print **border strips** to the top and bottom of the quilt top center to complete border 1.

Assemble Border 2

1. Select 2 different template A's from 1 of the 4 colors (for example, 1 light green print and 1 medium green print).
2. Matching right sides, sew 2 template A's together along one straight edge to make a **Quarter-Circle**.
3. Repeat Steps 1 and 2 to make quarter-circles in the remaining 3 colors.

Quarter-Circle

4. Select 4 template A's from each of the 4 prints of 1 color (for example, 1 each of the 4 green prints).

5. Matching right sides, sew 2 template A's together along one straight edge.

6. Sew the remaining 2 template A's to the first pieces to make a **Half-Circle**. Press seam allowances in one direction.

7. Repeat Steps 4 - 6 to make half-circles in the remaining 3 colors. You will have 2 template A's left over in each color.

Half-Circle

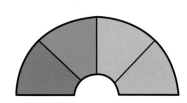

8. Referring to the **Border 2** diagram for placement, position the straight edges of the orange quarter-circle even with two adjacent edges of one 7$\frac{1}{2}$" x 50$\frac{1}{2}$" white print border strip at one end of the strip. Position the yellow quarter-circle at the opposite end of the same strip. Pin the quarter-circles in place. Satin Stitch appliqué the outer edges of the quarter-circles to the border strip. Repeat using the red and green quarter-circles and another 7$\frac{1}{2}$" x 50$\frac{1}{2}$" white print border strip.

9. Position 1 orange D over the orange quarter-circle and fuse in place. Repeat for the yellow, green, and red quarter-circles and the D's in the corresponding colors.

10. Satin Stitch appliqué the inner and outer edges of a D to each quarter-circle.

11. Sew these border strips to the long sides of the quilt top center. Press seam allowances toward border 1.

12. Align the short sides of one 7$\frac{1}{2}$" x 50$\frac{1}{2}$" border strip with the edges of the quilt top and then position the corresponding half-circles on the border strip. They should be aligned with the quarter-circle of the same color on the border strips you attached in Step 11. Pin the half-circles in place. Repeat for the remaining border strip and half-circles.

13. Satin Stitch appliqué the outer edges of the 4 half-circles to the border strips.

14. Position 1 C over each half-circle of the corresponding color, and fuse in place. Repeat for the remaining half-circles.

15. Satin Stitch appliqué the inner and outer edges of C to each half-circle.

16. Pin the top and bottom border strips to the quilt top, matching the inner and outer edges of the quarter-circles and half-circles, and then sew the borders in place to complete border 2. Press seam allowances toward border 1.

Border 2

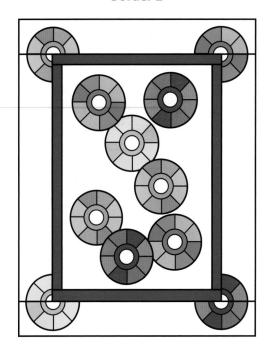

Assemble Border 3

1. Sew together one 2¹/₂" white print **strip** and one 2¹/₂" navy print strip to make a **Strip Set**. Make 8 strip sets.

Strip Set

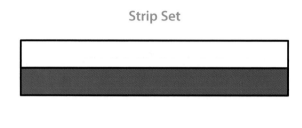

2. Refer to **Fig. 2** to cut these strip sets crosswise at 2¹/₂" intervals to make Unit 2. Cut 114 Unit 2's.

Fig. 2　　**Unit 2** (make 114)

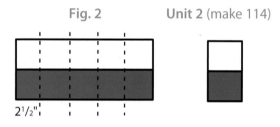

2¹/₂"

3. Sew 32 Unit 2's together (**Fig. 3**) to make one long side of the checkerboard border 3. Make 2 long sides.

Fig. 3

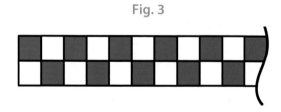

4. Sew the long sides of the border to the long sides of the quilt top.
5. Sew 25 Unit 2's together to make another checkerboard strip. Make 2 checkerboard strips of 25 Unit 2's each.
6. Sew one 4¹/₂" red print square to each end of a checkerboard strip to make the top and bottom **Border 3**. Make 2 border 3's.
7. Sew these border strips to the top and bottom of the quilt top to complete border 3.

Border 3

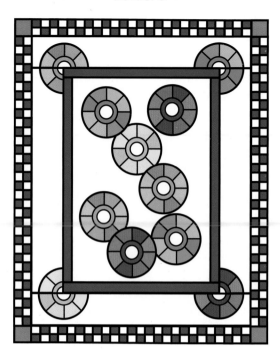

Assemble Border 4

1. Sew the 1¹/₂" x 72¹/₂" green print **border strips** to the long sides of the quilt top.
2. Sew the 1¹/₂" x 60¹/₂" green print border strips to the top and bottom of the quilt top to complete border 4.

Assemble Border 5

1. Sew the 2¹/₂" x 74¹/₂" yellow print strips to the long sides of the quilt top.
2. Sew one 2¹/₂" navy print **square** to each end of one 2¹/₂" x 60¹/₂" yellow print strip to make the top and bottom border 5.
3. Sew these border strips to the top and bottom of the quilt top to complete border 5.

Assemble Border 6

1. Divide the 2¹/₂" x 4¹/₂" **rectangles** into 4 groups, mixing the various colors and prints:
   - 2 groups of 39 rectangles each.
   - 2 groups of 32 rectangles each.
2. Referring to the **Quilt Top Diagram**, page 18, sew 39 rectangles together along their long sides to make the long sides of border 6. Make two border strips.
3. Sew the border strips to the long sides of the quilt top.

4. Sew 32 rectangles together along their long sides. Make two border strips.
5. Sew one 4¹/₂" navy print square to each end of one border strip. Make two of these to make the top and bottom strips of Border 6.
6. Sew the border strips to the top and bottom of the quilt top to complete Border 6.

COMPLETING THE QUILT

1. Follow **Quilting**, page 41, to mark, layer, and quilt as desired.
2. Refer to **Making a Hanging Sleeve**, page 45, to make and attach a hanging sleeve, if desired.
3. Using **binding strips**, follow **Binding**, page 45, to make and then attach straight-grain binding with mitered corners.

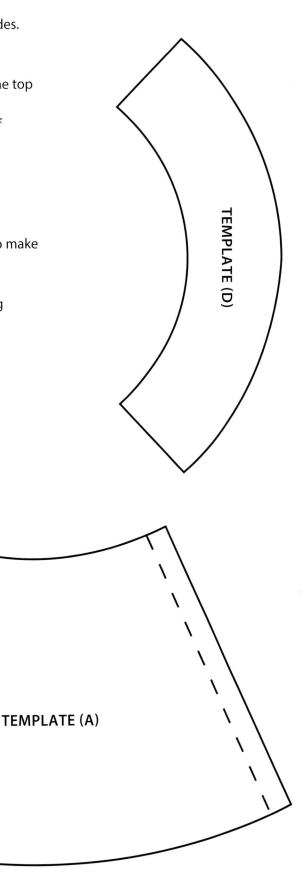

TEMPLATE (D)

TEMPLATE (A)

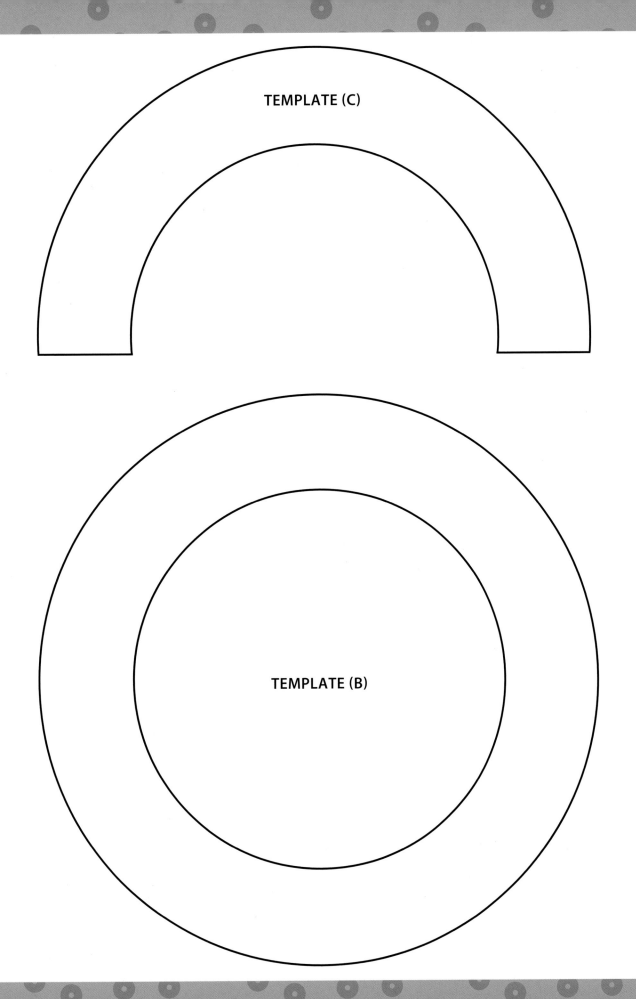

TEMPLATE (C)

TEMPLATE (B)

DRAGON'S TOOTH

Finished Quilt Size: 66" x 90" (168 cm x 229 cm)
Finished Block Size: 11" x 17" (28 cm x 43 cm)

SHOPPING LIST

Yardage is based on 43"/44" (109 cm/112 cm) wide fabric with a usable width of 40" (102 cm) after trimming selvages and shrinkage. A Fat Quarter is approximately 22" x 18" (56 cm x 46 cm).

- ☐ *16 fat quarters of assorted prints for blocks
- ☐ $1^7/_8$ yds (1.7 m) of pink print fabric for blocks and sashings
- ☐ $3^1/_8$ yds (2.9 m) of white solid fabric for blocks, sashings, and inner border
- ☐ $1^5/_8$ yds (1.5 m) of multi-color print fabric for outer border
- ☐ $5^1/_2$ yds (5 m) of fabric for backing
- ☐ $^3/_4$ yd (69 cm) of fabric for binding

You will also need:
- ☐ 74" x 98" (188 cm x 249 cm) piece of batting

* Fat quarters are required for directional prints. For non-directional prints, a Twice the Charms Roll or 16 strips $5^1/_2$" x 22" (14 cm x 56 cm) may be used instead.

Design by Sue Marsh for Whistlepig Creek Productions

CUTTING THE PIECES

Follow Rotary Cutting, page 37, to cut fabric. All measurements include $^1/_4$" seam allowances. Cut strips from fat quarters parallel to the short edges. Cut strips from Twice the Charm strips parallel to the long edges. Cut all strips from yardage from the selvage-to-selvage width of the fabric.

From *each* fat quarter:
- Cut 2 **wide strips** $5^1/_2$" x 11".

From pink print fabric:
- Cut 2 strips $15^1/_2$" wide. From these strips, cut 32 **side block sashings** $1^1/_2$" x $15^1/_2$".
- Cut 11 strips $1^1/_2$" wide. From these strips, cut 32 **top/bottom block sashings** $11^1/_2$" x $1^1/_2$".
- Cut 1 strip $3^1/_2$" wide. From this strip, cut 9 **sashing squares** $3^1/_2$" x $3^1/_2$".
- Cut 2 strips $1^1/_2$" wide. From these strips, cut 12 **sashing rectangles A** $3^1/_2$" x $1^1/_2$".
- Cut 1 strip $3^1/_2$" wide. From this strip, cut 12 **sashing rectangles B** $1^1/_2$" x $3^1/_2$".

From white solid fabric:
- Cut 8 **inner border strips** $1^1/_2$" wide.
- Cut 11 strips $3^1/_2$" wide. From these strips, cut 32 **medium strips** $3^1/_2$" x 11".
- Cut 11 strips $1^1/_2$" wide. From these strips, cut 32 **narrow strips** $1^1/_2$" x 11".
- Cut 10 strips $3^1/_2$" wide. From these strips, cut 24 **sashing rectangles C** $3^1/_2$" x $8^1/_2$" and 24 **sashing rectangles D** $3^1/_2$" x $5^1/_2$".

From multi-color print fabric:
- Cut 9 **outer border strips** $5^1/_2$" wide.

From fabric for binding:
- Cut 9 **binding strips** $2^1/_2$" wide.

MAKING THE BLOCKS

Follow Piecing, page 38, and Pressing, page 39, to make quilt top. Use ¼" seam allowances throughout.

1. Sew 1 **medium strip**, 1 **wide strip**, and 1 **narrow strip** together to make **Strip Set A**. Using matching wide strip and making sure direction of print is turned the same as in Strip Set A, sew 1 narrow strip, 1 wide strip, and 1 medium strip together to make **Strip Set B**. Cut along Strip Sets at 2" intervals to make 5 **Unit 1's** and 5 **Unit 2's**.

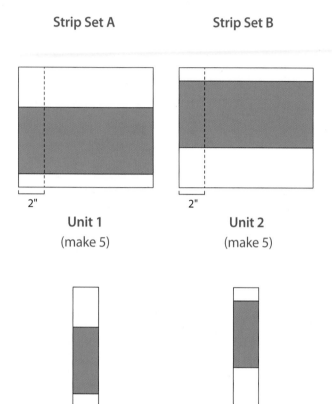

Strip Set A   **Strip Set B**

2"   2"

Unit 1   **Unit 2**
(make 5)   (make 5)

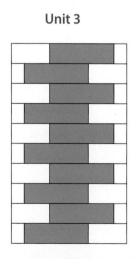

2. Sew 5 Unit 1's and 5 Unit 2's together to make **Unit 3**. Unit 3 should measure 9½" x 15½" including seam allowances.

Unit 3

3. Sew **side block sashings** and then **top/bottom block sashings** to Unit 3 to make **Block**. Block should measure 11½" x 17½" including seam allowances.

Block

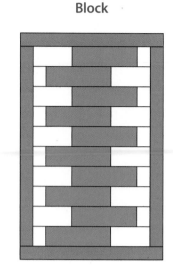

4. Repeat Steps 1-3 to make a total of 16 Blocks.

ASSEMBLING THE QUILT TOP CENTER

Refer to Quilt Top Diagram, page 25, to assemble quilt top.

1. Sew 1 **sashing rectangle A** and 2 **sashing rectangles C** together to make **vertical sashing**. Make 12 vertical sashings.

Vertical Sashing (make 12)

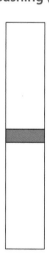

2. Sew 4 Blocks and 3 vertical sashings together to make **Row**. Row should measure 53$\frac{1}{2}$" x 17$\frac{1}{2}$" including seam allowances. Make 4 Rows.

Row (make 4)

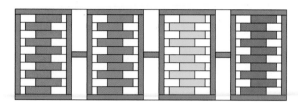

3. Sew 1 **sashing rectangle B** and 2 **sashing rectangles D** together to make **horizontal sashing**. Make 12 horizontal sashings.

Horizontal Sashing (make 12)

4. Sew 4 horizontal sashings and 3 **sashing squares** together to make **Sashing Row**. Sashing Row should measure 53$\frac{1}{2}$" x 3$\frac{1}{2}$" including seam allowances. Make 3 Sashing Rows.

Sashing Row (make 3)

5. Sew Rows and Sashing Rows together to make **Quilt Top Center**. Quilt Top Center should measure 53$\frac{1}{2}$" x 77$\frac{1}{2}$" including seam allowances.

ADDING THE BORDERS

1. Using diagonal seams (**Fig. 1**), sew **inner border strips** together end to end to make 1 continuous inner border strip.

Fig. 1

2. To determine length of **inner side borders**, measure length across center of quilt top center. From continuous inner border strip, cut 2 **inner side borders** the determined length. Matching centers and corners, sew **inner side borders** to quilt top center.

3. To determine length of **inner top/bottom borders**, measure width across center of quilt top center (including added borders). From continuous inner border strip, cut 2 **inner top/bottom borders** the determined length. Matching centers and corners, sew **inner top/bottom borders** to quilt top center.

4. In the same manner, use **outer border strips** to sew **outer borders** to Quilt Top.

COMPLETING THE QUILT

1. Follow **Quilting**, page 41, to mark, layer, and quilt as desired. Quilt shown is machine quilted with wavy lines in the blocks and a continuous loop pattern in the sashings and borders.

2. Follow **Making a Hanging Sleeve**, page 45, if a hanging sleeve is desired.

3. Use **binding strips** and follow **Binding**, page 45, to make and attach binding.

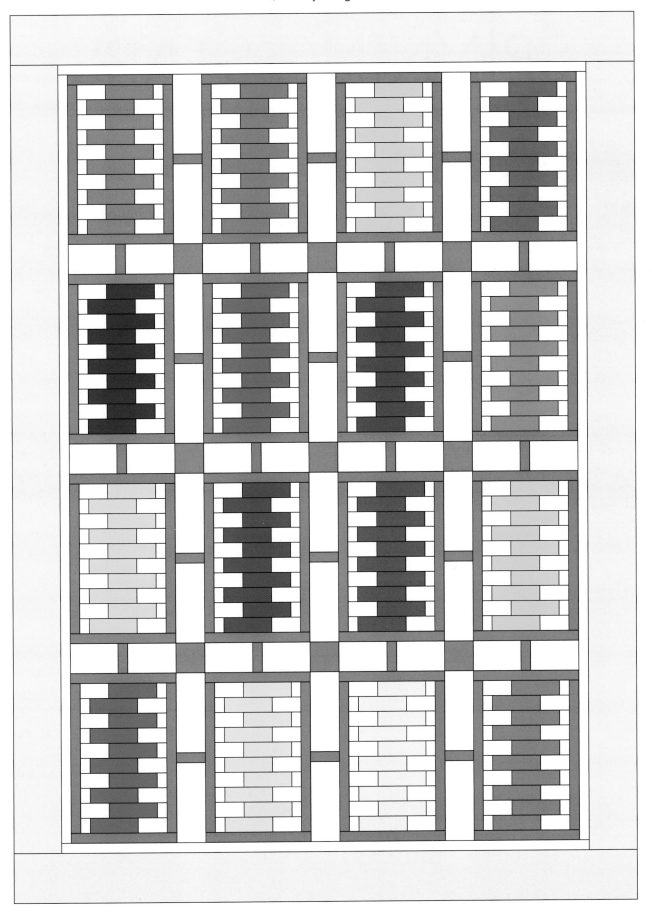

SPINNING STARS

Finished Quilt Size: 47¹⁄₈" x 60" (120 cm x 152 cm)

SHOPPING LIST

Yardage is based on 43"/44" (109 cm/112 cm) wide fabric with a usable width of 40" (102 cm) after trimming selvages and shrinkage.

- ☐ 1⁵⁄₈ yds (1.5 m) **total** of assorted print fabrics (background squares)
- ☐ 1³⁄₄ yds (1.6 m) of black print fabric (setting triangles, outer border, and binding)
- ☐ 1⁵⁄₈ yds (1.5 m) of white print fabric (inner border)
- ☐ Assorted scrap fabrics for appliqués
- ☐ 3⁷⁄₈ yds (3.5 m) of fabric for backing

You will also need:

- ☐ 55" x 68" (140 cm x 173 cm) piece of batting
- ☐ Paper-backed fusible web
- ☐ Stabilizer
- ☐ Matching 40 wt high-sheen polyester thread for appliqué stitching

Design by Linda Sullivan for
Linderella's Quilt Design Studio

CUTTING THE PIECES

*Follow **Rotary Cutting**, page 37, to cut fabric. Cutting lengths for borders are exact. You may wish to allow an extra 2" in length for "insurance" and then trim the borders to fit when you add them to the quilt top center. All measurements include ¹⁄₄" seam allowances.*

From assorted print fabrics:

- • Cut 18 appliqué background squares (**A**) 10" x 10".

From black print fabric:

- • Cut 2 *lengthwise* outer side borders (**B**) 3" x 54¹⁄₂".
- • Cut 2 *lengthwise* outer top/bottom borders (**C**) 3" x 46⁵⁄₈".
- • Cut 5 *lengthwise* binding strips (**D**) 2¹⁄₂" x 54".
- • Cut 2 squares 7³⁄₈" x 7³⁄₈". Cut each square once diagonally to make 4 Corner Setting Triangles (**E**).
- • Cut 3 squares 14" x 14". Cut each square twice diagonally to make 12 Setting Triangles (**F**). You will use 10; discard 2.

From white print fabric:

- • Cut 2 *lengthwise* inner side borders (**G**) 2" x 51¹⁄₂".
- • Cut 2 *lengthwise* inner top/bottom borders (**H**) 2" x 41⁵⁄₈".

CUTTING OUT THE APPLIQUÉS

*Refer to **Preparing Fusible Appliqués**, page 40, to make appliqués from patterns, page 30.*

From assorted scrap fabrics for appliqués:

- • Cut 18 large stars.
- • Cut 18 small stars.
- • Cut 18 star centers.

ASSEMBLING THE QUILT TOP

*Refer to **Satin Stitch Appliqué**, page 40, to add appliqués. Follow **Piecing**, page 38, and **Pressing**, page 39. Use a $^1/_4$" seam allowance throughout.*

1. Fuse and Satin Stitch 1 large star, 1 small star, and 1 star center to each appliqué background square (**A**). Trim squares to $9^1/_2$" x $9^1/_2$".
2. Refer to **Assembly Diagram** to assemble Quilt Top Center.
3. Leaving a $^1/_4$" seam allowance beyond where the blocks and setting triangles intersect, trim and square Quilt Top Center to $38^5/_8$" x $51^1/_2$".
4. Sew inner side borders (**G**) to Quilt Top Center. Sew inner top/bottom borders (**H**) to Quilt Top Center.
5. Sew outer side borders (**B**) to Quilt Top Center. Sew outer top/bottom borders (**C**) to Quilt Top Center.

COMPLETING THE QUILT

1. Follow **Quilting**, page 41, to mark, layer, and quilt as desired. Our quilt was stitched "in the ditch" around each appliqué and background square and along each border.
2. Refer to **Making a Hanging Sleeve**, page 45, to make and attach a hanging sleeve, if desired.
3. Follow **Binding**, page 45, to bind quilt using binding strips (**D**).

Assembly Diagram

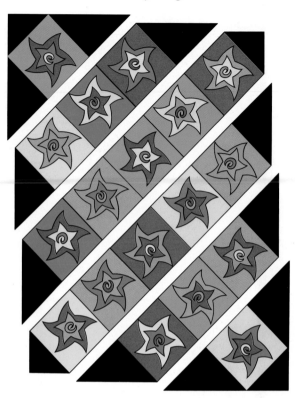

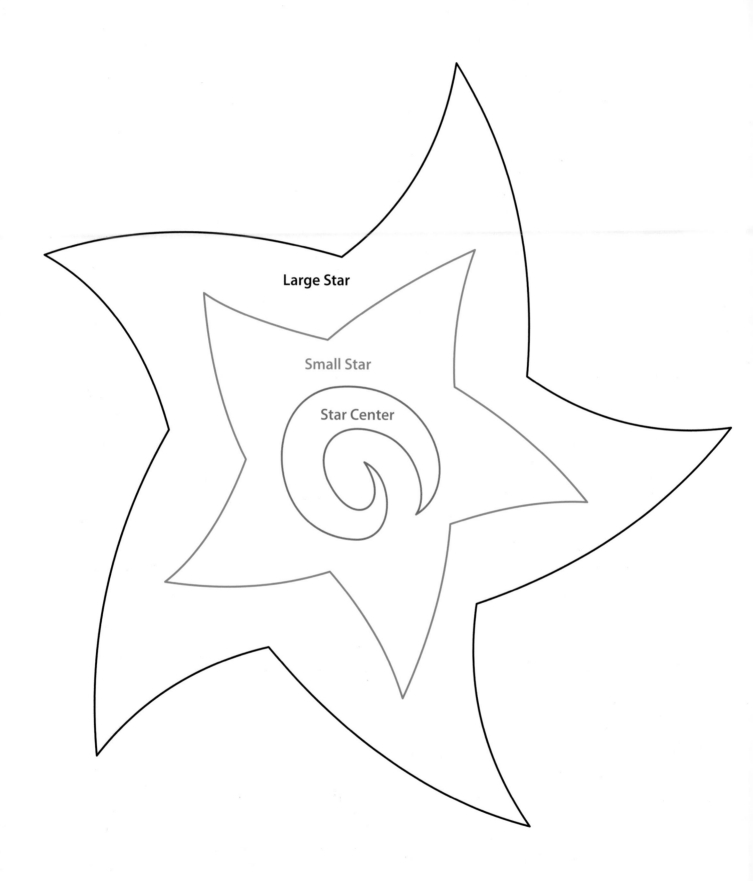

Large Star

Small Star

Star Center

STACKED CIRCLES

This bright quilt is made from bold colorful print fabrics and pieces cut from a retired military uniform. Uniform pieces show support and help family members at home feel close to their deployed loved ones.

Finished Quilt Size: 61" x 61" (155 cm x 155 cm)
Finished Block Size: 15" x 15" (38 cm x 38 cm)

SHOPPING LIST

Yardage is based on 43"/44" (109 cm/112 cm) wide fabric with a usable width of 40" (102 cm) after trimming selvages and shrinkage.

- ☐ 1 military uniform (shirt and pants) *or* 1³/₄ yds (1.6 m) of print fabric
- ☐ ¹/₂ yd (46 cm) *each* of 16 assorted print fabrics
- ☐ 2¹/₂ yds (2.3 m) of neutral color facing fabric
- ☐ 3⁷/₈ yds (3.5 m) of backing fabric
- ☐ ⁵/₈ yd (57 cm) of binding fabric

You will also need:
- ☐ 69" x 69" (175 cm x 175 cm) square of batting
- ☐ Template plastic
- ☐ Black fine-point permanent felt-tip pen
- ☐ Removable fabric marking pen or pencil

Design by Jen Eskridge
Machine quilted by Colleen Eskridge

CUTTING THE PIECES

Cut all strips across the selvage to selvage width of the fabric. All measurements include ¹/₄" seam allowances.

*From military uniform or print fabric:
- Cut 8 **large appliqué squares** 13" x 13".
- Cut 8 **small appliqué squares** 9" x 9".

From assorted print fabrics:
- Cut a *total* of 16 **background squares** 15¹/₂" x 15¹/₂".
- Cut a *total* of 8 **large appliqué squares** 13" x 13".
- Cut a *total* of 8 **small appliqué squares** 9" x 9".

From facing fabric:
- Cut 6 strips 13" wide. From these strips, cut 16 **facing squares** 13" x 13".

From binding fabric:
- Cut 7 **binding strips** 2¹/₂" wide.

*Before cutting, remove any buttons, zippers, and insignia from the uniform pieces. Do not remove pockets. Squares should be cut to include pieces of pockets and seams.

Continued on page 32.

Stacked Circles continued.

MAKING THE QUILT TOP

*Match right sides and raw edges and use a 1/4" seam allowance unless otherwise noted. Follow **Template Cutting**, page 38, to make templates from small and large circle patterns, page 35.*

1. Using the large circle template, uniform fabric **large appliqué squares**, print fabric **large appliqué squares**, and **facing squares**, follow **Making Closed Appliqués**, page 36, to make 16 **large closed appliqués**.

Large Closed Appliqué (make 16)

2. Using the small circle template, uniform fabric **small appliqué squares**, print fabric **small appliqué squares**, and facing fabric circles left over from the centers of large closed appliqués, make 16 **small closed appliqués**.

Small Closed Appliqué (make 16)

3. Randomly arrange 1 large and 1 small circle appliqué on 1 **background square**; pin.
4. Stitching 1/8" from faced edges, topstitch large and small circles to background square to make **Block**. Make 16 Blocks.

Block (make 16)

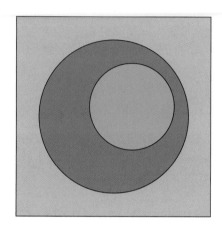

5. Sew 4 Blocks together to make a **Row**. Make 4 Rows.
6. Sew Rows together to make the **Quilt Top**.

COMPLETING THE QUILT

1. Follow **Quilting**, page 41, to mark, layer, and quilt as desired. The model is machine quilted with all-over meandering quilting.
2. If desired, follow **Making A Hanging Sleeve**, page 45, to make and attach a hanging sleeve.
3. Use **binding strips** and follow **Binding**, page 45, to make and attach **straight-grain binding**.

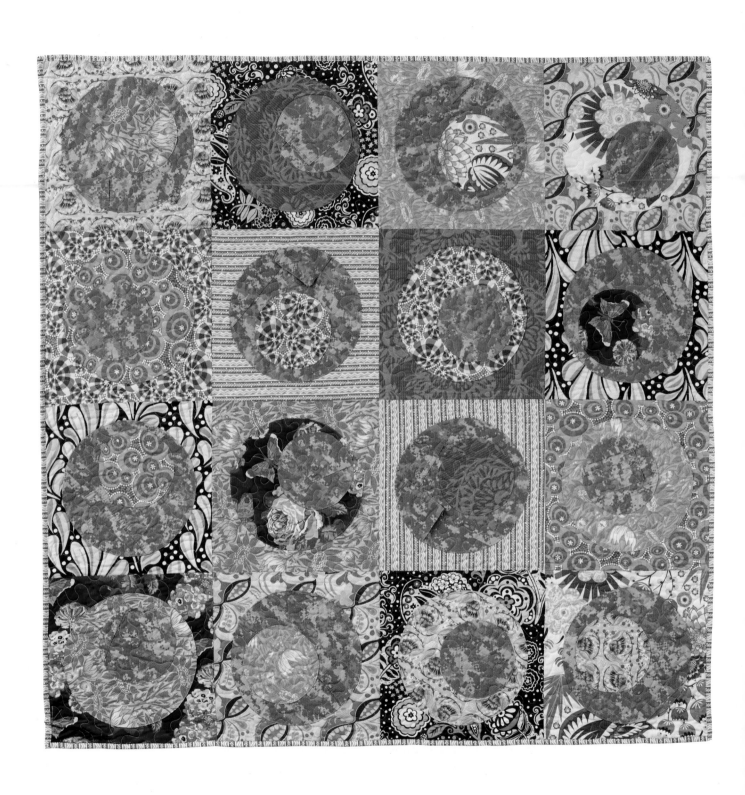

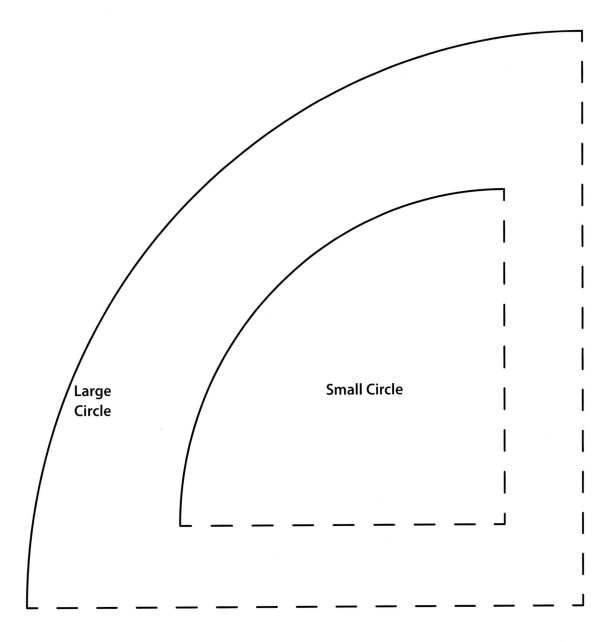

Large Circle

Small Circle

To trace a complete circle pattern, trace quarter pattern onto template plastic. Rotate plastic $1/4$ turn and trace pattern again. Continue rotating and tracing until a complete circle is traced.

MAKING CLOSED APPLIQUÉS

*The entire outer edge of a Closed Appliqué is faced, as viewed from the wrong side in **Fig. 1**.*

Fig. 1

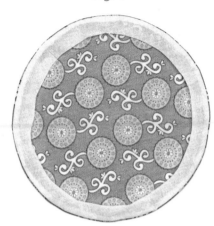

1. Use the **templates**, **appliqué squares**, and **facing squares** called for in your project instructions when making Closed Appliqués.
2. Draw around the template on the wrong side of the facing square.
3. Matching right sides and raw edges, pin 1 appliqué square and 1 facing square together. Stitch exactly on the drawn line (**Fig. 2**).

Fig. 2

TIP: Using a slow stitch speed and a shorter stitch length will make sewing circles and tight curves easier.

4. Make a small snip in the facing fabric 1" from the stitched line. Insert the scissors into the opening; trim facing to 1" (**Fig. 3**).

Fig. 3

5. Trim the appliqué fabric seam allowance to $1/4$" and the facing fabric seam allowances to $1/8$". Notch the seam allowances by snipping small V's of fabric out of the seam allowances; snip up to but not through the stitching line.
6. Turn the facing to the wrong side and press the appliqué from the facing side, allowing a tiny bit of the appliqué fabric to roll to the wrong (facing) side to complete a **Closed Appliqué**.

Closed Appliqué

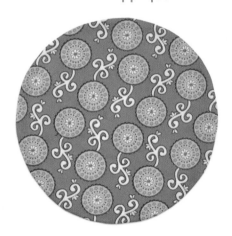

GENERAL INSTRUCTIONS

To make your quilting easier and more enjoyable, we encourage you to carefully read all of the general instructions, study the color photographs, and familiarize yourself with the individual project instructions before beginning a project.

FABRICS

SELECTING FABRICS

Choose high-quality, medium-weight 100% cotton fabrics. All-cotton fabrics hold a crease better, fray less, and are easier to quilt than cotton/polyester blends.

Yardage requirements listed for each project are based on 43"/44" wide fabric with a "usable" width of 40" after shrinkage and trimming selvages. Actual usable width will probably vary slightly from fabric to fabric. Our recommended yardage lengths should be adequate for occasional re-squaring of fabric when many cuts are required.

PREPARING FABRICS

We recommend that all fabrics be washed, dried, and pressed before cutting. If fabrics are not pre-washed, washing the finished quilt will cause shrinkage and give it a more "antiqued" look and feel. Bright and dark colors, which may run, should always be washed before cutting. After washing and drying fabric, fold lengthwise with wrong sides together and matching selvages.

ROTARY CUTTING

- Place fabric on work surface with fold closest to you.

- Cut all strips from the selvage-to-selvage width of the fabric unless otherwise indicated in project instructions.

- Square left edge of fabric using rotary cutter and rulers (**Figs. 1-2**).

Fig. 1

Fig. 2

- To cut each strip required for a project, place ruler over cut edge of fabric, aligning desired marking on ruler with cut edge; make cut (**Fig. 3**).

Fig. 3

- When cutting several strips from a single piece of fabric, it is important to make sure that cuts remain at a perfect right angle to the fold; square fabric as needed.

- Many precut fabrics have pinked edges and most manufacturers include the points of the pinked edges in the measurement given on the label. Before cutting precuts into smaller pieces, measure your precuts to determine if you need to include the points to achieve the correct cut size.

TEMPLATE CUTTING

Our template patterns have a solid cutting line.

1. To make a template from a pattern, use a permanent fine-point pen and a ruler to carefully trace the solid line on the pattern onto template plastic. Cut out template along inner edge of drawn line. Check template against original pattern for accuracy.
2. Place template face down on wrong side of fabric. Use a sharp fabric-marking pencil to draw around template. Cut out fabric piece using scissors.

PIECING

Precise cutting, followed by accurate piecing, will ensure that all the pieces of the quilt top fit together well.

- Set sewing machine stitch length for approximately 11 stitches per inch.

- Use neutral-colored general-purpose sewing thread (not quilting thread) in needle and in bobbin.

- An accurate $1/4$" seam allowance is essential. Presser feet that are $1/4$" wide are available for most sewing machines.

- For an accurate seam allowance when piecing precuts with pinked edges, measure from point to point across the center of the piece. If it measures the exact size, align the tip of the points with your $1/4$" seam guide when sewing. It may be necessary to use a "scant" $1/4$" seam allowance. Making a "test block" will determine if any adjustments to your seam allowances are necessary.

- When piecing, always place pieces right sides together and match raw edges; pin if necessary.

- Chain piecing saves time and will usually result in more accurate piecing.

- Trim away points of seam allowances that extend beyond edges of sewn pieces.

SEWING STRIP SETS

When there are several strips to assemble into a strip set, first sew strips together into pairs, then sew pairs together to form strip set. To help avoid distortion, sew seams in opposite directions **(Fig. 4)**.

Fig. 4

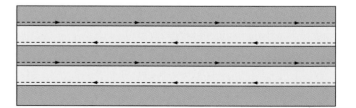

SEWING ACROSS SEAM INTERSECTIONS

When sewing across intersection of two seams, place pieces right sides together and match seams exactly, making sure seam allowances are pressed in opposite directions (**Fig. 5**).

Fig. 5

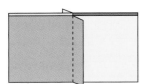

SEWING SHARP POINTS

To ensure sharp points when joining triangular or diagonal pieces, stitch across the center of the "X" (shown in pink) formed on wrong side by previous seams (**Fig. 6**).

Fig. 6

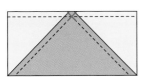

PRESSING

• Use steam iron set on "Cotton" for all pressing.

• Press after sewing each seam.

• Seam allowances are almost always pressed to one side, usually toward the darker fabric. However, to reduce bulk it may occasionally be necessary to press seam allowances toward the lighter fabric or even to press them open.

• To prevent dark fabric seam allowance from showing through light fabric, trim darker seam allowance slightly narrower than lighter seam allowance.

• To press long seams, such as those in long strip sets, without curving or other distortion, lay strips across width of the ironing board.

• When sewing blocks into rows, seam allowances may be pressed in one direction in odd numbered rows and in the opposite direction in even numbered rows. When sewing rows together, press seam allowances in one direction.

APPLIQUÉ

Preparing Fusible Appliqués

White or light-colored fabrics may need to be lined with fusible interfacing before applying fusible web to prevent darker fabrics from showing through.

1. Place paper-backed fusible web, paper side up, over appliqué pattern. Trace pattern onto paper side of web with pencil as many times as indicated in project instructions for a single fabric.

2. Follow manufacturer's instructions to fuse traced patterns to wrong side of fabrics. Do not remove paper backing. *(Note: Some pieces may be given as measurements, such as a 2" x 4" rectangle, instead of drawn patterns. Fuse web to wrong side of fabrics indicated for these pieces.)*

3. Use scissors to cut out appliqué pieces along traced lines; use rotary cutting equipment to cut out appliqué pieces given as measurements. Remove paper backing from all pieces.

Satin Stitch Appliqué

A good satin stitch is a thick, smooth, almost solid line of zigzag stitching that covers the exposed raw edges of appliqué pieces.

1. Pin stabilizer, such as paper or any of the commercially available products, on wrong side of background fabric before stitching appliqués in place.

2. Thread sewing machine with general-purpose or high-sheen polyester thread; use general-purpose or high-sheen polyester thread that matches background fabric in bobbin.

3. Set sewing machine for a medium (approximately $1/8$") zigzag stitch and a short stitch length. Slightly loosening the top tension may yield a smoother stitch.

4. Begin by stitching two or three stitches in place (drop feed dogs or set stitch length at 0) to anchor thread. Most of the Satin Stitch should be on the appliqué with the right edge of the stitch falling at the outside edge of the appliqué. Stitch over all exposed raw edges of appliqué pieces.

5. *(Note: Dots on **Figs. 7-12** indicate where to leave needle in fabric when pivoting.)* For outside corners, stitch just past corner, stopping with needle in background fabric (**Fig. 7**). Raise presser foot. Pivot project, lower presser foot, and stitch adjacent side (**Fig. 8**).

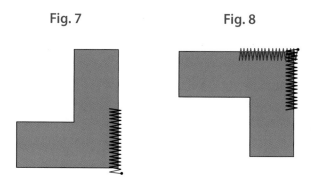

Fig. 7   Fig. 8

6. For inside corners, stitch just past corner, stopping with needle in appliqué fabric (**Fig. 9**). Raise presser foot. Pivot project, lower presser foot, and stitch adjacent side (**Fig. 10**).

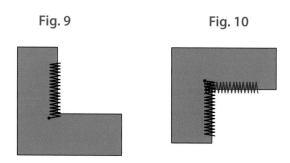

Fig. 9   Fig. 10

7. When stitching outside curves, stop with needle in background fabric. Raise presser foot and pivot project as needed. Lower presser foot and continue stitching, pivoting as often as necessary to follow curve (**Fig. 11**).

Fig. 11

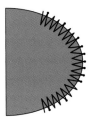

8. When stitching inside curves, stop with needle in appliqué fabric. Raise presser foot and pivot project as needed. Lower presser foot and continue stitching, pivoting as often as necessary to follow curve (**Fig. 12**).

Fig. 12

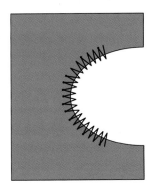

9. Do not backstitch at end of stitching. Pull threads to wrong side of background fabric; knot thread and trim ends.
10. Carefully tear away stabilizer.

QUILTING

*Quilting holds the three layers (top, batting, and backing) of the quilt together and can be done by hand or machine. Because marking, layering, and quilting are interrelated and may be done in different orders depending on circumstances, please read entire **Quilting** section, pages 41-44, before beginning project.*

TYPES OF QUILTING DESIGNS

In the Ditch Quilting
Quilting along seamlines or along edges of appliquéd pieces is called "in the ditch" quilting. This type of quilting should be done on side **opposite** seam allowance and does not have to be marked.

Outline Quilting
Quilting a consistent distance, usually $1/4$", from seam or appliqué is called "outline" quilting. Outline quilting may be marked, or $1/4$" masking tape may be placed along seamlines for quilting guide. (Do not leave tape on quilt longer than necessary, since it may leave an adhesive residue.)

Motif Quilting
Quilting a design, such as a feathered wreath, is called "motif" quilting. This type of quilting should be marked before basting quilt layers together.

Echo Quilting
Quilting that follows the outline of an appliquéd or pieced design with two or more parallel lines is called "echo" quilting. This type of quilting does not need to be marked.

Channel Quilting
Quilting with straight, parallel lines is called "channel" quilting. This type of quilting may be marked or stitched using a guide.

Crosshatch Quilting

Quilting straight lines in a grid pattern is called "crosshatch" quilting. Lines may be stitched parallel to edges of quilt or stitched diagonally. This type of quilting may be marked or stitched using a guide.

Meandering Quilting

Quilting in random curved lines and swirls is called "meandering" quilting. Quilting lines should not cross or touch each other. This type of quilting does not need to be marked.

Stipple Quilting

Meandering quilting that is very closely spaced is called "stipple" quilting. Stippling will flatten the area quilted and is often stitched in background areas to raise appliquéd or pieced designs. This type of quilting does not need to be marked.

MARKING QUILTING LINES

Quilting lines may be marked using fabric marking pencils, chalk markers, or water- or air-soluble pens.

Simple quilting designs may be marked with chalk or chalk pencil after basting. A small area may be marked, then quilted, before moving to next area to be marked. Intricate designs should be marked before basting using a more durable marker.

Caution: Pressing may permanently set some marks. **Test** different markers **on scrap fabric** to find one that marks clearly and can be thoroughly removed.

A wide variety of precut quilting stencils, as well as entire books of quilting patterns, are available. Using a stencil makes it easier to mark intricate or repetitive designs.

To make a stencil from a pattern, center template plastic over pattern and use a permanent marker to trace pattern onto plastic. Use a craft knife with single or double blade to cut channels along traced lines (**Fig. 13**).

Fig. 13

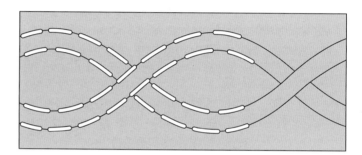

PREPARING THE BACKING

To allow for slight shifting of quilt top during quilting, backing should be approximately 4" larger on all sides. Yardage requirements listed for quilt backings are calculated for 43"/44"w fabric. Using 90"w or 108"w fabric for the backing of a bed-sized quilt may eliminate piecing. To piece a backing using 43"/44"w fabric, use the following instructions.

1. Measure length and width of quilt top; add 8" to each measurement.
2. If determined width is 79" or less, cut backing fabric into two lengths slightly longer than determined length measurement. Trim selvages. Place lengths with right sides facing and sew long edges together, forming tube (**Fig. 14**). Match seams and press along one fold (**Fig. 15**). Cut along pressed fold to form single piece (**Fig. 16**).

| Fig. 14 | Fig. 15 | Fig. 16 |

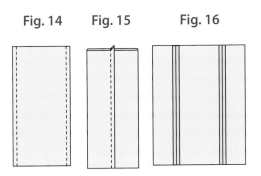

3. If determined width is more than 79", it may require less fabric yardage if the backing is pieced horizontally. Divide determined length measurement by 40" to determine how many widths will be needed. Cut required number of widths the determined *width* measurement. Trim selvages. Sew long edges together to form single piece.
4. Trim backing to size determined in Step 1; press seam allowances open.

CHOOSING THE BATTING

The appropriate batting will make quilting easier. For fine hand quilting, choose low-loft batting. All cotton or cotton/polyester blend battings work well for machine quilting because the cotton helps "grip" quilt layers. If quilt is to be tied, a high-loft batting, sometimes called extra-loft or fat batting, may be used to make quilt "fluffy."

Types of batting include cotton, polyester, wool, cotton/polyester blend, cotton/wool blend, and silk.

When selecting batting, refer to package labels for characteristics and care instructions. Cut batting same size as prepared backing.

ASSEMBLING THE QUILT

1. Examine wrong side of quilt top closely; trim any seam allowances and clip any threads that may show through front of the quilt. Press quilt top, being careful not to "set" any marked quilting lines.
2. Place backing *wrong* side up on flat surface. Use masking tape to tape edges of backing to surface. Place batting on top of backing fabric. Smooth batting gently, being careful not to stretch or tear. Center quilt top *right* side up on batting.
3. Use 1" rustproof safety pins to "pin-baste" all layers together, spacing pins approximately 4" apart. Begin at center and work toward outer edges to secure all layers. If possible, place pins away from areas that will be quilted, although pins may be removed as needed when quilting.

MACHINE QUILTING METHODS

Use general-purpose thread in bobbin. Do not use quilting thread. Thread the needle of machine with general-purpose thread or transparent monofilament thread to make quilting blend with quilt top fabrics. Use decorative thread, such as a metallic or contrasting-color general-purpose thread, to make quilting lines stand out more.

Straight-Line Quilting

The term "straight-line" is somewhat deceptive, since curves (especially gentle ones) as well as straight lines can be stitched with this technique.

1. Set stitch length for six to ten stitches per inch and attach walking foot to sewing machine.
2. Determine which section of quilt will have longest continuous quilting line, oftentimes area from center top to center bottom. Roll up and secure each edge of quilt to help reduce the bulk, keeping fabrics smooth. Smaller projects may not need to be rolled.
3. Begin stitching on longest quilting line, using very short stitches for the first 1/4" to "lock" quilting. Stitch across project, using one hand on each side of walking foot to slightly spread fabric and to guide fabric through machine. Lock stitches at end of quilting line.
4. Continue machine quilting, stitching longer quilting lines first to stabilize quilt before moving on to other areas.

Free-Motion Quilting

Free-motion quilting may be free form or may follow a marked pattern.

1. Attach darning foot to sewing machine and lower or cover feed dogs.
2. Position quilt under darning foot; lower foot. Holding top thread, take a stitch and pull bobbin thread to top of quilt. To "lock" beginning of quilting line, hold top and bobbin threads while making three to five stitches in place.
3. Use one hand on each side of darning foot to slightly spread fabric and to move fabric through the machine. Even stitch length is achieved by using smooth, flowing hand motion and steady machine speed. Slow machine speed and fast hand movement will create long stitches. Fast machine speed and slow hand movement will create short stitches. Move quilt sideways, back and forth, in a circular motion, or in a random motion to create desired designs; do not rotate quilt. Lock stitches at end of each quilting line.

MAKING A HANGING SLEEVE

Attaching a hanging sleeve to back of wall hanging or quilt before the binding is added allows project to be displayed on wall.

1. Measure width of quilt top edge and subtract 1". Cut piece of fabric 7"w by determined measurement.
2. Press short edges of fabric piece $1/4$" to wrong side; press edges $1/4$" to wrong side again and machine stitch in place.
3. Matching wrong sides, fold piece in half lengthwise to form tube.
4. Follow project instructions to sew binding to quilt top and to trim backing and batting. Before Blindstitching binding to backing, match raw edges and stitch hanging sleeve to center top edge on back of quilt.
5. Finish binding quilt, treating hanging sleeve as part of backing.
6. Blindstitch bottom of hanging sleeve to backing, taking care not to stitch through to front of quilt.
7. Insert dowel or slat into hanging sleeve.

BINDING

Binding encloses the raw edges of the quilt. Because of its stretchiness, bias binding works well for binding projects with curves or rounded corners and tends to lie smooth and flat in any given circumstance. Binding may also be cut from straight lengthwise or crosswise grain of fabric.

MAKING STRAIGHT-GRAIN BINDING

1. To determine length of strip needed if attaching binding with mitered corners, measure edges of quilt and add 12".
2. To determine lengths of strips needed if attaching binding with overlapped corners, measure each edge of quilt; add 3" to each measurement.
3. Cut lengthwise or crosswise strips of binding fabric the determined length and the width called for in project instructions. Strips may be pieced to achieve necessary length.
4. Matching wrong sides and raw edges, press strip(s) in half lengthwise to complete binding.

ATTACHING BINDING WITH MITERED CORNERS

1. Beginning with one end near center on bottom edge of quilt, lay binding around quilt to make sure that seams in binding will not end up at a corner. Adjust placement if necessary. Matching raw edges of binding to raw edge of quilt top, pin binding to right side of quilt along one edge.

2. When you reach first corner, mark ¹/₄" from corner of quilt top (**Fig. 17**).

Fig. 17

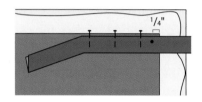

3. Beginning approximately 10" from end of binding and using ¹/₄" seam allowance, sew binding to quilt, backstitching at beginning of stitching and at mark (**Fig. 18**). Lift needle out of fabric and clip thread.

Fig. 18

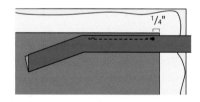

4. Fold binding as shown in **Figs. 19-20** and pin binding to adjacent side, matching raw edges. When you've reached the next corner, mark ¹/₄" from edge of quilt top.

Fig. 19   Fig. 20

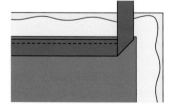   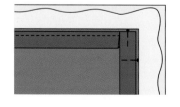

5. Backstitching at edge of quilt top, sew pinned binding to quilt (**Fig. 21**); backstitch at the next mark. Lift needle out of fabric and clip thread.

Fig. 21

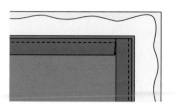

6. Continue sewing binding to quilt, stopping approximately 10" from starting point (**Fig. 22**).

Fig. 22

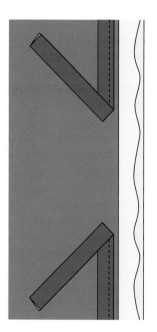

7. Bring beginning and end of binding to center of opening and fold each end back, leaving a ¼" space between folds (**Fig. 23**). Finger press folds.

Fig. 23

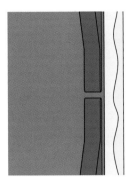

8. Unfold ends of binding and draw a line across wrong side in finger-pressed crease. Draw a line through the lengthwise pressed fold of binding at the same spot to create a cross mark. With edge of ruler at cross mark, line up 45° angle marking on ruler with one long side of binding. Draw a diagonal line from edge to edge. Repeat on remaining end, making sure that the two diagonal lines are angled the same way (**Fig. 24**).

Fig. 24

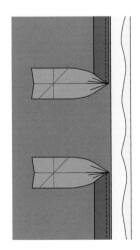

9. Matching right sides and diagonal lines, pin binding ends together at right angles (**Fig. 25**).

Fig. 25

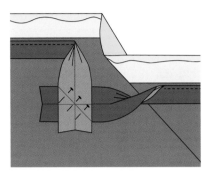

10. Machine stitch along diagonal line (**Fig. 26**), removing pins as you stitch.

Fig. 26

11. Lay binding against quilt to double check that it is correct length.
12. Trim binding ends, leaving ¼" seam allowance; press seam open. Stitch binding to quilt.
13. If using 2½"w binding (finished size ½"), trim backing and batting a scant ¼" larger than quilt top so that batting and backing will fill the binding when it is folded over to quilt backing. If using narrower binding, trim backing and batting even with edges of quilt top.

14. On one edge of quilt, fold binding over to quilt backing and pin pressed edge in place, covering stitching line (**Fig. 27**). On adjacent side, fold binding over, forming a mitered corner (**Fig. 28**). Repeat to pin remainder of binding in place.

Fig. 27   Fig. 28

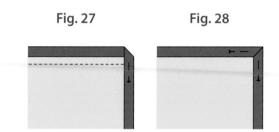

15. Blindstitch binding to backing (**Fig. 29**), taking care not to stitch through to front of quilt.

Fig. 29

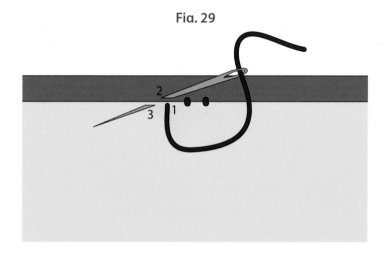

SIGNING AND DATING YOUR QUILT

A completed quilt is a work of art and should be signed and dated. There are many different ways to do this and numerous books on the subject. The label should reflect the style of the quilt, the occasion or person for which it was made, and the quilter's own particular talents. Following are suggestions for recording the history of quilt or adding a sentiment for future generations.

- Embroider quilter's name, date, and any additional information on quilt top or backing. Matching floss, such as cream floss on white border, will leave a subtle record. Bright or contrasting floss will make the information stand out.

- Make label from muslin and use permanent marker to write information. Use different colored permanent markers to make label more decorative. Stitch label to back of quilt.

- Use photo-transfer paper to add image to white or cream fabric label. Stitch label to back of quilt.

- Piece an extra block from quilt top pattern to use as label. Add information with permanent fabric pen. Appliqué block to back of quilt.